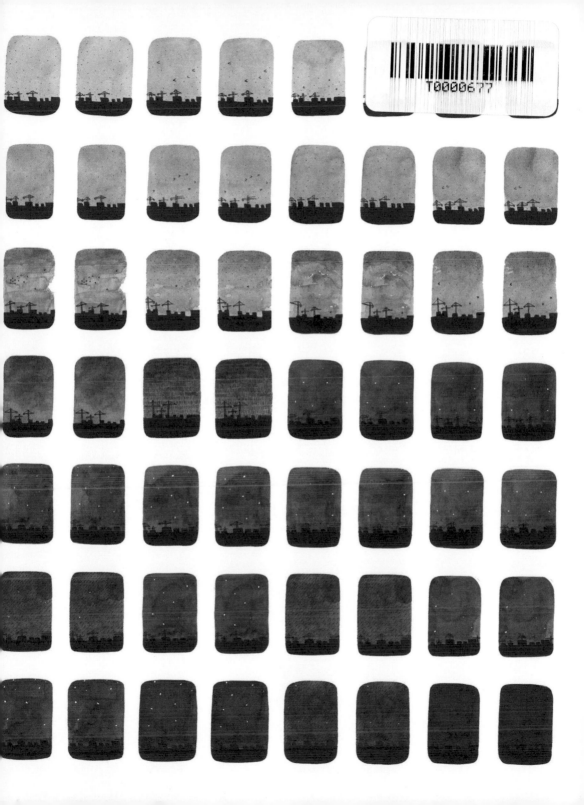

THE BOOK OF
MOONS&
SEASONS

Hannah McDonald

LIMINAL 11

LIMINAL 11

First published in 2022 by Liminal 11

Editorial Director: Darren Shill
Art Director: Kay Medaglia
Editor and Designer: Tori Jones
Cover Design: Jing Lau

Printed in China

ISBN 978-1-912634-40-8
10 9 8 7 6 5 4 3 2 1

www.liminal11.com

This book is dedicated to Noah and Emiliano, may we spend all seasons together.

And to our Mother Earth, may we follow your seasons to learn your wisdom and treat you better.

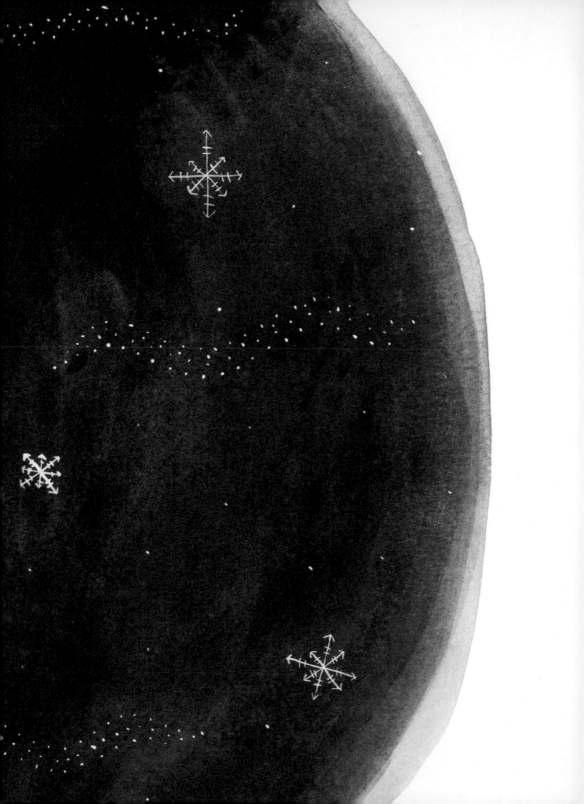

Winter solstice

The land is dark and still,
cold winds sweep
from the east.
Small creatures are
hiding in their holes
and burrows,
whilst plants and
trees wield
power in their roots
underground.
This is the darkest
day of the year.

Orion hunts
the winter sky.

A WINTER STORY,
OR WHEN THE SKY FILLED WITH STARS

Crisp winter
nights,
clear, cold
and dark.

Bright stars
shining above,

Orange windows

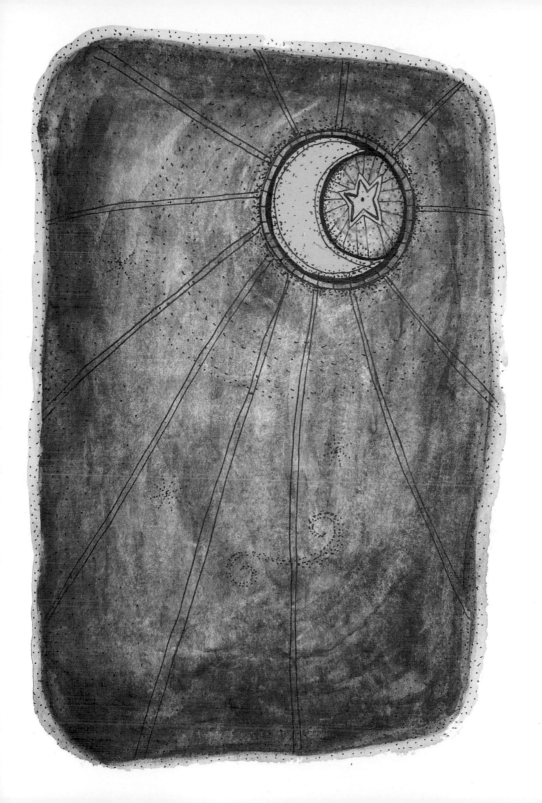

The cold bites my fingers.

There are moments

of warmth from the sun.

Winter days can be beautiful,

I think to myself.

But, as though hearing my thoughts,

the sun is hidden by a cloud

and all becomes covered in a cold stone gray.

The darkness reminding me it is still here.

Wolf Moon

Moon of January

The full moon in January is often referred to as the Wolf Moon. This is a folk name given both by the Native Americans and the Medieval Europeans. This moon is named after the wolves our ancestors would hear howling during this winter month. Once thought to be the sound of hungry beasts circling the villages, it is now believed that wolves howl more around this time of year to attract mates. Other names given to this full moon include Old Moon, Moon After Yule and Ice Moon.

MONDAY 7:42 AM

TUESDAY 7:27 AM

WEDNESDAY 7:17 AM

SUNDAY 7:27 AM

MONDAY 7:31 AM

TUESDAY 7:28 AM

SATURDAY 7:43 AM

SUNDAY 7:28 AM

MONDAY 7:42 AM

THURSDAY 7:18 AM

FRIDAY 7:28 AM

SATURDAY 7:43 AM

WEDNESDAY 7:19 AM

THURSDAY 7:21 AM

FRIDAY 7:28 AM

TUESDAY 7:43 AM

WEDNESDAY 7:27 AM

THURSDAY 7:23 AM

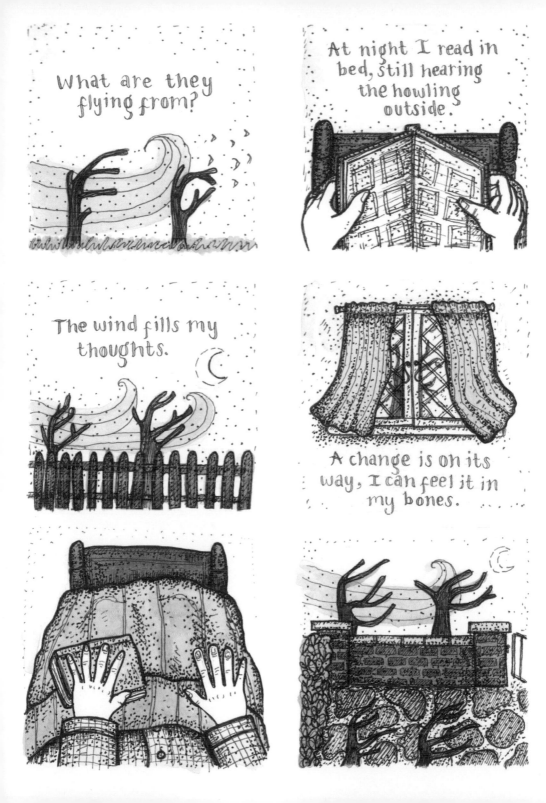

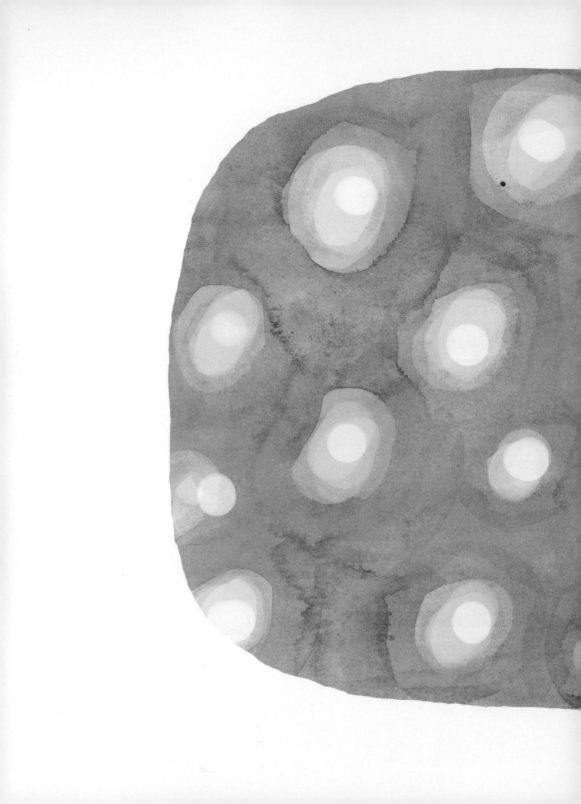

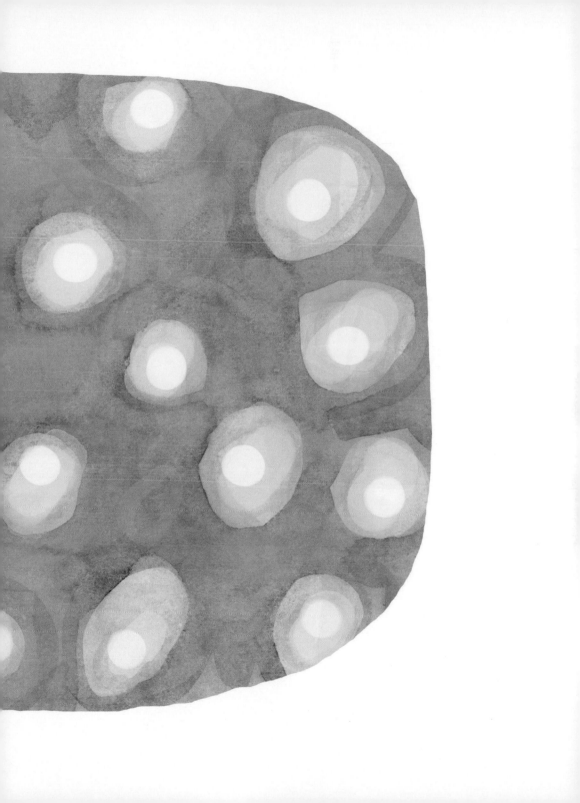

snow moon

moon of february

The Native American name for
the full moon in February is the
Snow Moon, as this is the time of year
when snowfall is at its heaviest in the
Northern Hemisphere. The Snow Moon
would have offered our ancestors some
much-needed light and comfort during
this cold, dark month.
Other folk names for this month's full
moon include Hunger Moon, Bone Moon
and Storm Moon.
The month of February is also home to
the festival of Imbolc which celebrates
the half way point between the
Winter Solstice and the Spring
Equinox.

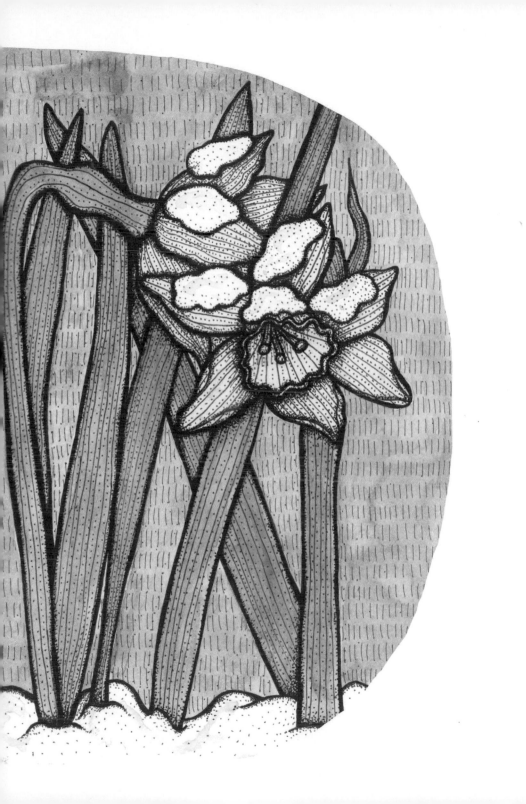

Imbolc

Walking today,
I see snowdrops coming up,
looking so delicate
against the roughness
of winter.

"Hold on," they sing.
"We bring
news
from
the green
goddess below.
She is slowly waking
from her slumber
and soon will rise."

I celebrate this news,
for warmth and color
are on the way.

Yet Winter's gray presence
interrupts my thoughts,
"But not yet!" he cries.
"Spring must wait her turn.
My time is still here,
and I'm not finished yet!"

MONDAY 7:42 AM

TUESDAY 7:27 AM

WEDNESDAY 7:17 AM

SUNDAY 7:27 AM

MONDAY 7:31 AM

TUESDAY 7:28 AM

SATURDAY 7:43 AM

SUNDAY 7:28 AM

MONDAY 7:42 AM

THURSDAY 7:18 AM

FRIDAY 7:28 AM

SATURDAY 7:43 AM

WEDNESDAY 7:19 AM

THURSDAY 7:21 AM

FRIDAY 7:28 AM

TUESDAY 7:43 AM

WEDNESDAY 7:27 AM

THURSDAY 7:23 AM

The garden has some color

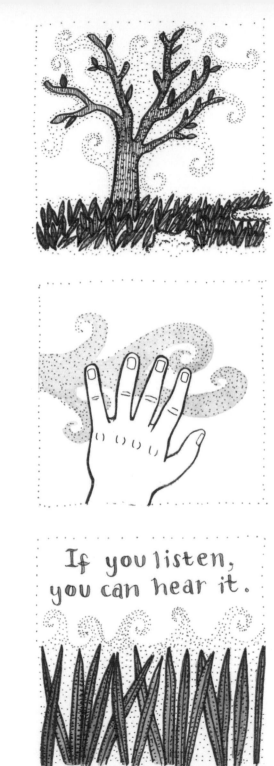

after months of brown and grays.

An energy is rising now.

If you listen, you can hear it.

A buzz of excitement.

"Something is coming,"

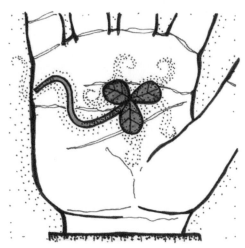

the energy is saying.

"And when it arrives,

worm moon

moon of March

The full moon in March is sometimes referred to as the Worm Moon, a name given by the Native Americans. The name is inspired by the return of earthworms to the soil's surface at this time of year, as the warmer weather thaws the frosts of winter. Other folk names for this moon include Sap Moon, Crow Moon, Chaste Moon and Crust Moon.

The Spring Equinox occurs around the 21st of March each year. This serves as a marker to celebrate the day and night nearing equal length once more, and the astronomical start of Spring.

Spring Equinox

As quickly as winter arrives,
he leaves,
and spring awakens
with such abundance

it's hard to believe
she was ever gone at all.

Maybe her spirit
was always here
throughout the dark winter,
leaving us signs of the
greenness ahead.

Continuously pushing on
against the Winter,
the Spring balances
the darkness with the light.
They are now equal.
Blossoms open
and bees awaken.

There is a slowness outside,
I no longer need to rush
home to warmth,
out here feels just fine.
The garden, my old friend.

A SPRING STORY,
OR WHEN THE SWANS DISAPPEARED

The most
I have
seen at
one time is
twenty-three.

whilst they float
in the water.

I often wonder if they sometimes wake up not knowing where they are after floating too far away in their sleep.

And I start
to wonder if they
have disappeared
forever.

But overnight,
around the
same time
each summer,
they reappear.
Gliding along,
cygnets
in tow.

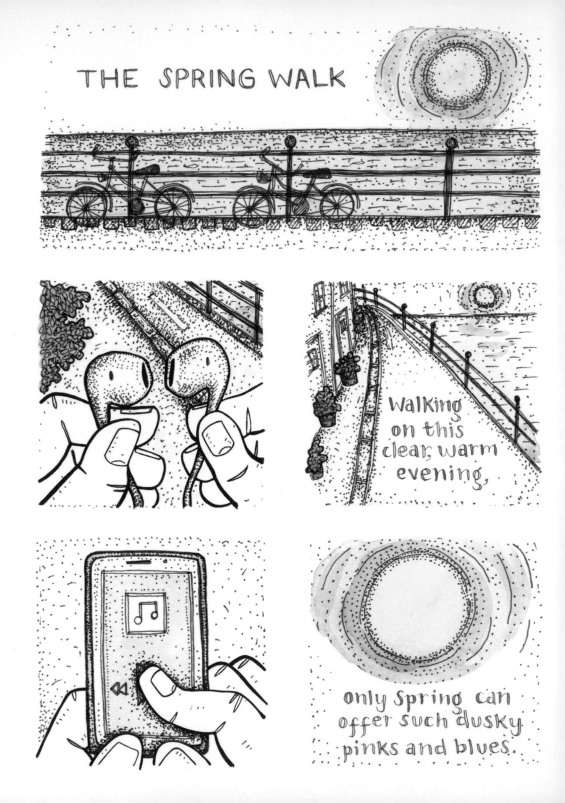

No sweltering heat of summer,

nor the cold darkness of Winter,

but the moment when things feel in balance,

at peace,

a calm ease.

Anything could happen,

when Spring magic is at work.

Apparently, there will be a meteor shower tonight,

Cassiopeia the queen
reigns over the
Spring sky.

The full moon in April has traditionally been called the Seed Moon. With the last frosts gone and the soil ready for sowing, this is the best month to plant vegetable seeds. The days are now longer than during the winter months and allow for more time lazing about outside watching the garden grow.

Other names for this moon include Pink Moon, after the pink Phlox flowers that bloom around this time of the year, Sprouting Grass Moon, Fish Moon and Egg Moon.

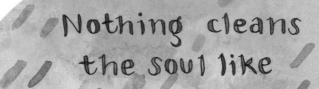

Nothing cleans
the soul like

a walk in the
fresh spring rain.

The swallows

arrive,

back for spring,

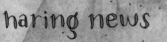haring news

of their travels

as they fly.

The
feel
of
grass

and
sand
underfoot

will
soon be
upon us.

A walk to see the bluebells in the woods.

Flower Moon

Moon of May

The full moon in May was called the Flower Moon by some Native Americans. This name refers to the abundance of flowers that bloom during this month. Other names for this moon include Hare Moon, Milk Moon and Corn Planting Moon. The old Celtic festival of Beltane is held at the beginning of May to celebrate the abundance and fertility of nature at this time of year due to the warmer, longer days. This festival also marks the halfway point between the Spring Equinox and the Summer Solstice.

Beltane

The green goddess has woken,
a warmth in the air
where there used to be cool blue.

The time
of darkness
is waning,
and now
is the turn of
the light
to keep us well
and help the plants
to grow.

Now the warmth
wakes the flowers
who sing their songs to the sun.
I light the Beltane fire.

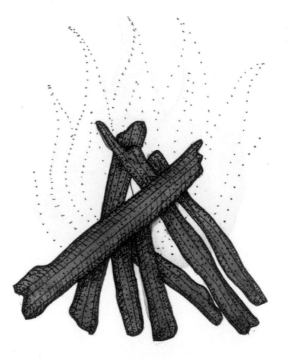

The insects and birds return,
gliding on the cool spring breeze.
The raindrops fall onto
the lush green leaves.
Spring is at her peak,
raise up your face,
forget your coat
and enjoy.

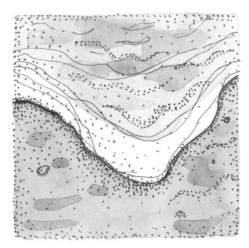

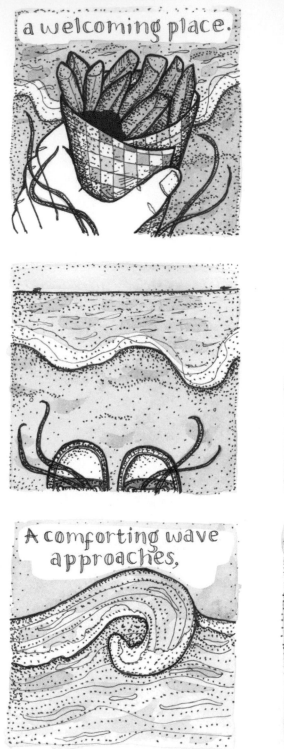

strawberry Moon

Moon of June

The full moon in June has been called the Strawberry Moon, as this is the month when strawberries tend to ripen. An alternate name for this moon is Rose Moon, a name of European origin, thought to come from the roses that bloom bountifully at this time of year.

Other names for this moon include Mead Moon, Hot Moon and Honey Moon. June also plays host to the Summer Solstice, around the 21st.

This festival celebrates the longest day of the year and the astronomical start of summer.

LAZING IN THE GARDEN

The green blades of grass,

swaying in the breeze.

not a cloud.

Sitting in the garden,

not doing anything.

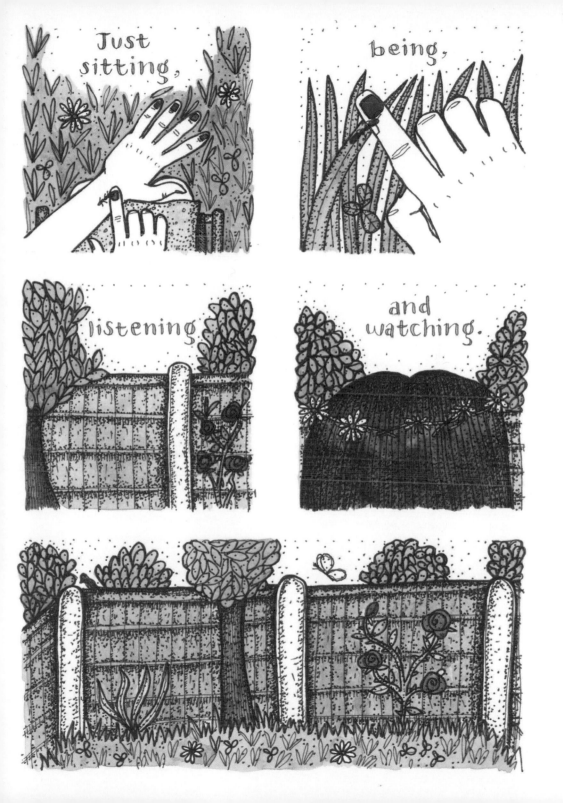

Summer Solstice

The longest day
of the year,
full of light.

Be outside and feel the
sun's energy.

We celebrate Today
and all that she brings.

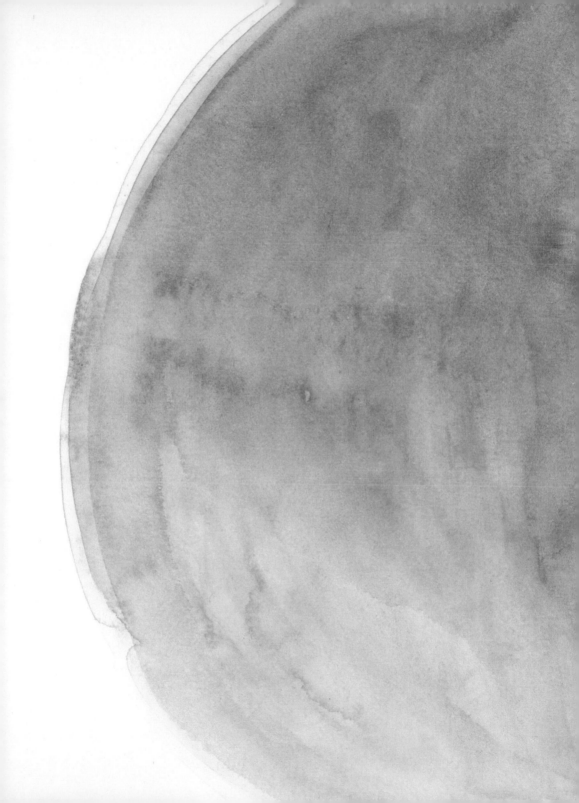

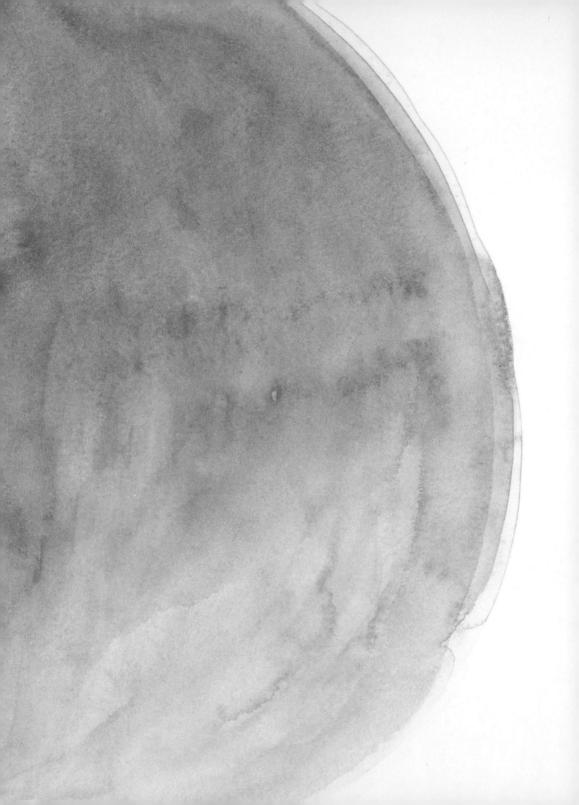

Tomorrow we will
begin the slow
return to the dark.
But first, we
have the long days
of summer to enjoy.

A SUMMER STORY,
OR WHEN WE HAD DINNER
IN THE GARDEN

Long summer evenings, a magical gift of extra time.

We have our dinner in the garden amongst the rose bushes and weeping willows.

Wearing no shoes, we feel the cool grass between our toes

and
listen to
the quiet
hum of

insects
and toads
croaking,

while
the last
of the
starlings
sing.

Hanging
glass jars
with tea
lights are
lit,

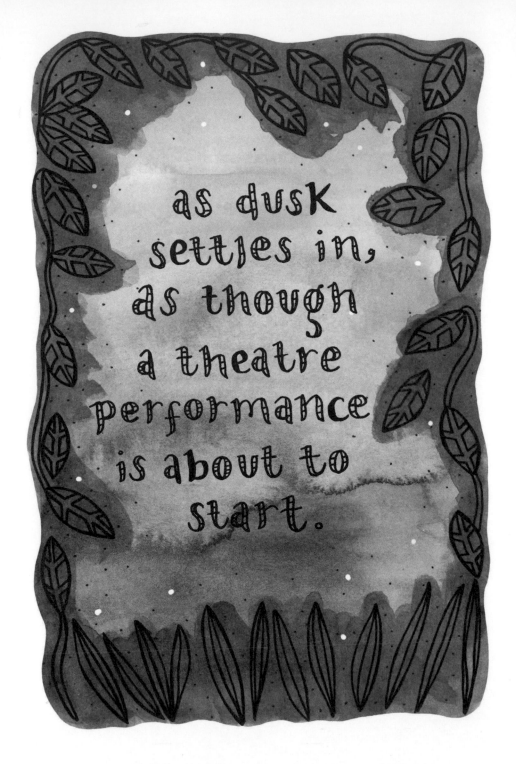

as dusk settles in, as though a theatre performance is about to start.

Aquila flies
high in the
summer sky.

BUCK MOON

Moon of July

The Native American name for the full moon in July is the Buck Moon, as this is the time of year when male deer's antlers regrow. This is also known as the Hay Moon as July is a time when hay is cut, bundled and stored by farmers, ready to be used throughout the winter months.

Another name for this moon is the Thunder Moon.

THE BEACH SELLER

Sitting on the sand,

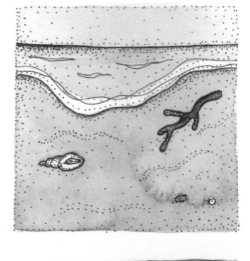

watching the lady with long dark hair

and bells on her skirt

as she wanders across the beach,

from one side to the other.

Selling the jewelry

made from shells she's found.

She moves with the sun

and takes breaks under the shady trees.

MONDAY 7:42 AM

TUESDAY 7:27 AM

WEDNESDAY 7:17 AM

SUNDAY 7:27 AM

MONDAY 7:31 AM

TUESDAY 7:28 AM

SATURDAY 7:43 AM

SUNDAY 7:28 AM

MONDAY 7:42 AM

THURSDAY 7:18 AM

FRIDAY 7:28 AM

SATURDAY 7:43 AM

WEDNESDAY 7:19 AM

THURSDAY 7:21 AM

FRIDAY 7:28 AM

TUESDAY 7:43 AM

WEDNESDAY 7:27 AM

THURSDAY 7:23 AM

Grain Moon

Moon of August

The full moon in August has traditionally been dubbed the Grain Moon, thought to be named so because many crops and grains can begin to be harvested at this time of year. Other names for this moon include Sturgeon Moon and Green Corn Moon. The Celtic festival of Lughnasadh happens early this month and celebrates both the beginning of the harvest and the mid point between the Summer Solstice and the Autumn Equinox.

Lammas

The blackberries are starting to ripen,

I pick them from the path

at the back of my house.

I think of the farmers now
And how they must feel looking
over fields of food they've grown.

The beginning of their harvest,

I celebrate with a homemade loaf.

Kneading dough like my ancestors,

Who would have been busy

at this time of year, collecting

all that they'd grown.

I will continue to pick blackberries
when I see them and enjoy this
time of harvest.

Heavy summer storms,

coming down from
the heavens.

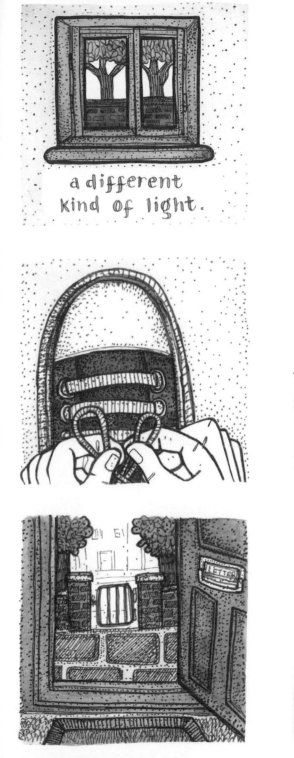

A return to routine

after timeless days of summer.

The storm last night

cleared out the muggy heat

and with it the feeling

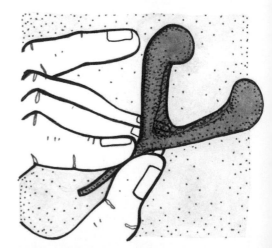

Harvest Moon

Moon of September

The full moon in September is often referred
to as the Harvest Moon, a European name.
The Harvest Moon is so named because, before
the modern age, its shine would allow farmers
to work longer into the night, harvesting the last
of their crops before the cold weather arrived.
The Autumn Equinox occurs towards the end of
this month and celebrates the second point
annually when the days and nights are
nearly equal in length. Now, with this event
marking the beginning of autumn, the days
darken and the nights begin to lengthen once
more. The Harvest Moon title is given to the
full moon closest to the Autumn Equinox, which
mostly occurs in September but takes place
in October every three years. Other names
for this moon include Corn Moon and Barley
Moon.

Autumn Equinox

A golden sun melting into
a golden sky,
glittering across the water.
Crisp air, cool and clear.

Frost now seems possible after
the long sun-filled months.
The smell of fires being lit,
brown leaves, coffee
and dewy grass.

Dreams of walking in forests
with hot chocolate
and knitted scarves.

The new season begins

with a bang of joy and gold.

A preview of the colors to come.

AN AUTUMNAL STORY,

OR WHEN I WENT FOR A

WALK IN THE WOODS

On
autumnal
mornings
the woods
call out
to me,

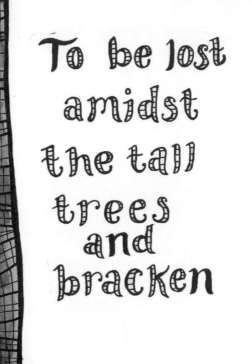

To be lost
amidst
the tall
trees
and
bracken

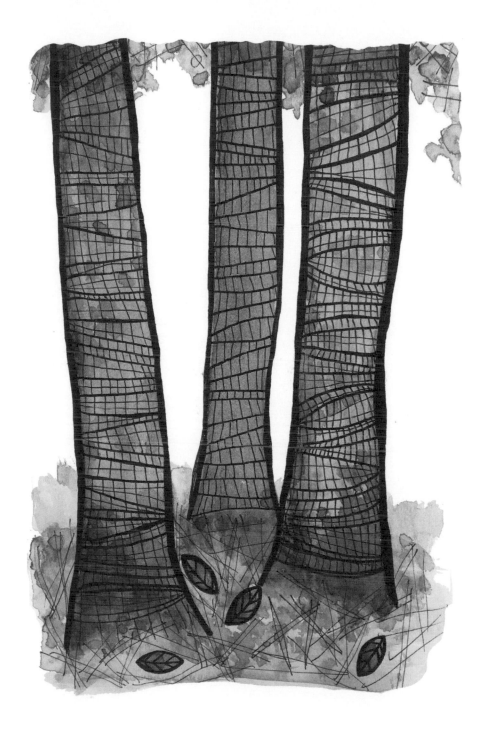

whilst feeling
the comfort of
a home I have

known
for
centuries.

The birds
Sing out to
each other,

warning
of movement
below their perch.

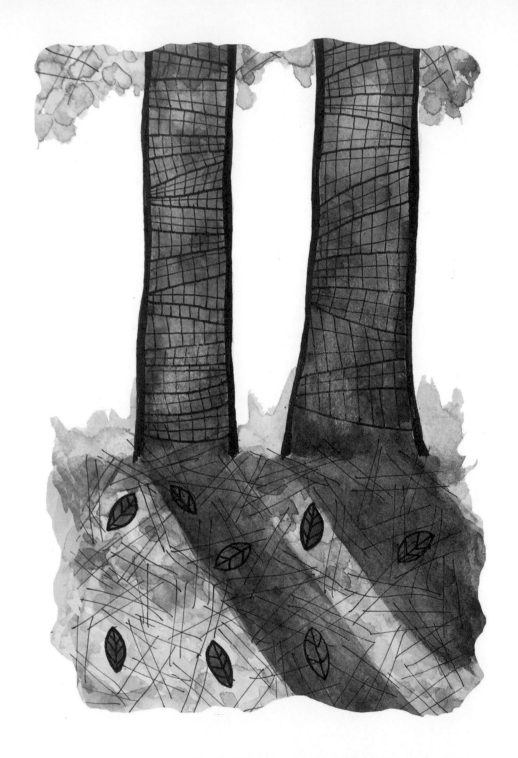

Small creatures hide, keeping their secrets from me.

I wander
onwards
until I hear
a new call,
of home
and a warm
cup of tea.

DARK MORNINGS

I feel the magic of the dark mornings.

Candles can be lit

and the moment felt,

Hunter's moon

Moon of October

One name for the full moon
in October is the Hunter's Moon
as this is the time of year people
would traditionally go hunting to
prepare for the dark, cold months ahead.
Every two or three years, there is an extra
full moon in the lunar calendar. When this
happens, the second full moon of the month
is called the Blue Moon. At the end of this
month is the Celtic festival of Samhain. Samhain
marks the end of the harvest season and
the beginning of the darker part of the year.
This is also the midpoint between the
Autumn Equinox and the Winter Solstice.
Other names for the full moon in October
are Blood Moon, Dying Grass Moon and
Travel Moon.

Pegasus rides
across the
autumn sky.

Every now
and then, there
is an extra full
moon in a month.
This is the
Blue Moon.
So, most years there
are twelve full
there is a Blue
are

noons, but when
Moon, there
thirteen.

Samhain

The wind blows down the street
Blustering through
Leaves and branches.
Scarves and hair fly,
Whilst cheeks chill and redden.

"Pay attention,"
The wind calls,
"For now is the
   Moment for change."

A time to reflect and look inwards.
I read my cards
On this dark Samhain night.

The veil is thin,
And messages can be heard.
"The end is near," they read.
"Rebirth will come again,
But first we must prepare to rest."

HALLOWEEN NIGHT

The evening falls dark early today,

and a chill lingers in the air.

The wind has been howling for hours,

whispering words of change.

I close my eyes and listen.

"Follow me," it says.

The candle flickers,

the upstairs window opens and closes.

The wind blows through the branches

and the moon looks down over the eerie land.

Beaver moon

moon of November

The full moon in November has traditionally been called the Beaver Moon, a Native American name.

Some believe it came from the creation of beaver traps during this month, others from the many beavers rushing to make their dams before the winter sets in. Another name for this moon is the Frost or Frosty moon.

MONDAY 7:42 AM

TUESDAY 7:27 AM

WEDNESDAY 7:17 AM

SUNDAY 7:27 AM

MONDAY 7:31 AM

TUESDAY 7:28 AM

SATURDAY 7:43 AM

SUNDAY 7:28 AM

MONDAY 7:42 AM

THURSDAY 7:18 AM

FRIDAY 7:28 AM

SATURDAY 7:43 AM

WEDNESDAY 7:19 AM

THURSDAY 7:21 AM

FRIDAY 7:28 AM

TUESDAY 7:43 AM

WEDNESDAY 7:27 AM

THURSDAY 7:23 AM

THE MOUNTAINS IN AUTUMN

Watching a golden sun sink,

behind the peaks up high.

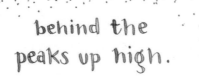

The snow
glistening
orange,

whilst dark
pine trees
stand
tall,

as though
protecting
the slope.

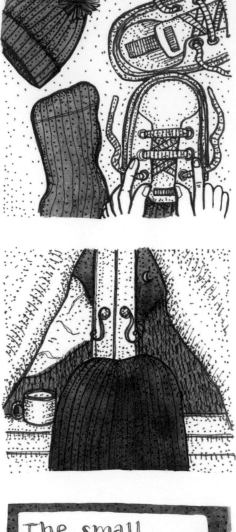

Soon the valley will be dark.

The small houses will glow,

cold moon

moon of December

The Native American name for the full moon in December is the Cold Moon, due to its position at the beginning of the biting season of winter. Other names for this moon include Long Night Moon, Oak Moon and Full Cold Moon. The Winter Solstice, which occurs around the 21st of this month, marks both the shortest day of the year and the astronomical start of winter. The Solstice is traditionally a time of celebration. Although it is the darkest point in the year, it means that light will soon return once again.

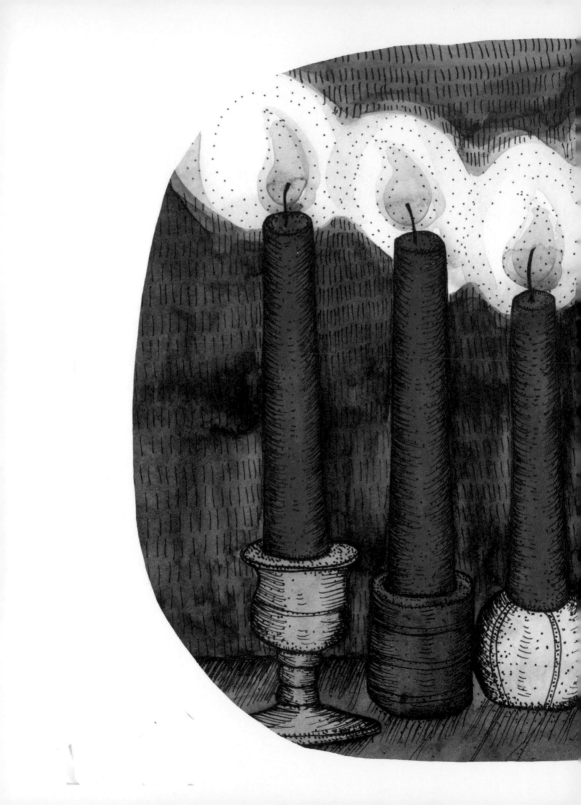

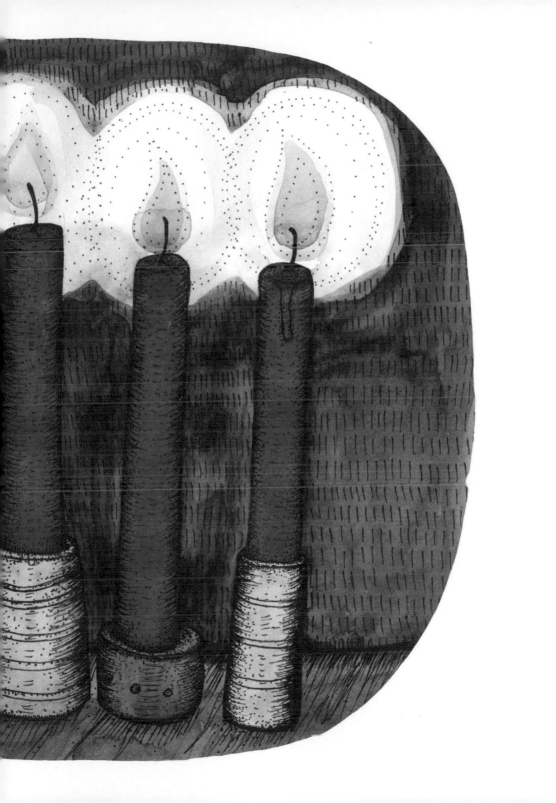

And so, another
year ends.
The days and
nights darken,
so we celebrate
together

with candlelight
and green
holly and pine,
and walk into the
new year with
smiles on our faces.

Winter solstice

There is a stillness to the shortest
day of the year. It is a time to celebrate
the transition from old to new. Both
moving forward and thinking of
times long past.
Would our ancestors have feared
the days getting darker and darker,
perhaps they thought the light
would never return?
Or were they too intuitively aware
of the cyclic turning of the year?
We can now celebrate that this is the
darkest the world will be, and sunshine
will return. It's time to be inside, to stay
cozy and keep warm, in deep reflection.
There is a stillness to the shortest
day of the year.

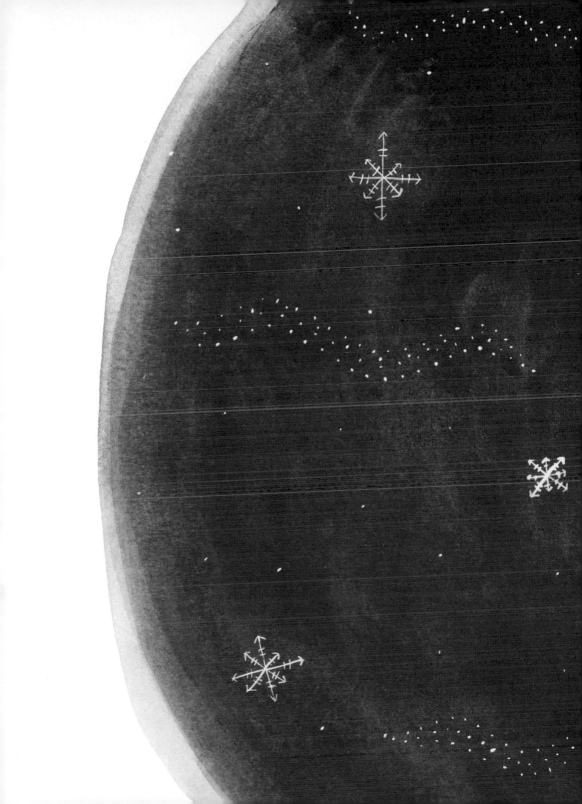

Works Consulted

www.history.com
www.nationalgeographic.co.uk
www.space.com
solarsystem.nasa.gov
www.almanac.com

Seasons of the Moon: Folk Names and Lore of the Full Moon
by Michael Carabetta

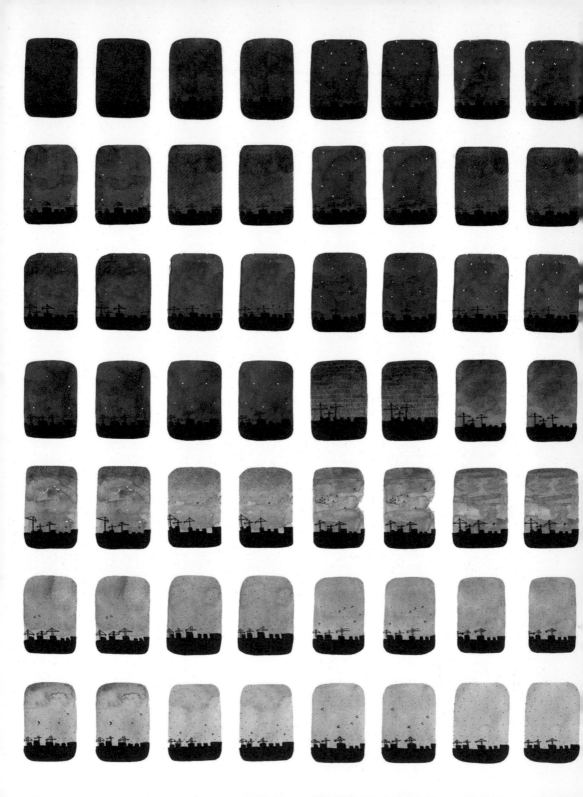